SEA REPTILES

BY
S.L. HAMILTON

A&D Xtreme
An imprint of Abdo Publishing | abdopublishing.com

Printed in the United States of America, North Mankato, MN.
092017
012018

THIS BOOK CONTAINS
RECYCLED MATERIALS

Editor: John Hamilton
Graphic Design: Sue Hamilton
Cover Design: Candice Keimig and Pakou Vang
Cover Photo: iStock
Interior Photos & Illustrations: Alamy-pgs 11 (inset), 14-15, 16-17 & 24-25; AP-pgs 6-7, 10-11 & 14 (inset); Getty-pgs 4-5 & 8-9; Glow Images-pg 1; Science Source-pgs 18-19, 22-23 & 28-29; Shutterstock-pgs 2-3, 12-13, 16 (inset), 17 (inset), 20-21 & 30-31; Royal Tyrrell Museum-pg 32; Smithsonian Institute-pgs 26-27.

Publisher's Cataloging-in-Publication Data

Names: Hamilton, S.L., author.
Title: Sea reptiles / by S.L. Hamilton.
Description: Minneapolis, Minnesota : Abdo Publishing, 2018. |
      Series: Xtreme Dinosaurs | Includes online resources and index.
Identifiers: LCCN 2017946717 | ISBN 9781532112973 (lib.bdg.) |
      ISBN 9781532150838 (ebook)
Subjects: LCSH: Marine reptiles, Fossil--Juvenile literature. |
      Prehistoric animals--Juvenile literature. | Dinosaurs--Juvenile
      literature. | Paleontology--Juvenile literature.
Classification: DDC 567.937--dc23
LC record available at https://lccn.loc.gov/2017946717

CONTENTS

SEA REPTILES

Tylosaurus
(Knob Lizard)

Sea reptiles were not dinosaurs, but lived at the same time. Ichthyosaurs, plesiosaurs, pliosaurs, and mosasaurs swam in Earth's seas during the Mesozoic era. They breathed air like today's whales.

These powerful swimmers had jaws filled with sharp teeth. They easily hunted their fill of large sharks, squid, fish, and even flying reptiles and sea birds. For millions of years, marine reptiles ruled the prehistoric seas.

XTREME FACT – A sea reptile was one of the first fossil reptiles ever correctly identified. An ichthyosaur was found by Mary and Joseph Anning in Great Britain in 1811.

TEETH

Sea reptiles had jaws filled with teeth. Some had teeth designed for grasping and holding prey. Small-toothed sea reptiles ate soft prey, such as squid. Others had interlocking teeth that trapped prey in the reptile's mouth. Some big-headed sea reptiles had dagger-like teeth that allowed them to grab and eat larger meals, such as crocodiles, turtles, and other hard-shelled sea creatures.

A few sea reptiles had long pointed jaws with only a few teeth. They likely swung their heads back and forth, using the jaw much like today's swordfish. They then collected and ate the pieces of their prey.

XTREME FACT – Plesiosaur fossils have been found with dozens of stones in their bodies. The sea reptiles swallowed these "gastroliths" to help break up and digest the large pieces of food they ate.

EYES

Sea reptiles had excellent eyesight. Fossils show a well-developed sclerotic ring. This doughnut-shaped bone surrounding the eye kept the sea reptile's eyeball from losing its shape. Even when swimming fast or diving to great depths, their vision stayed sharp to hunt prey or escape from predators.

Ophthalmosaurus
(Eye Lizard)

XTREME FACT – Ophthalmosaurus ("Eye Lizard") was an ichthyosaur with eyes the size of grapefruit. Its huge eyes allowed in lots of light, much like today's owls. This meant it could dive to great depths, where there was little light, and still find food.

ICHTHYOSAURS

Ichthyosaurs swam in Earth's seas 240 million to 93 million years ago. Their name means "fish lizard." They had smooth bodies and looked something like dolphins.

Cymbospondylus
(Boat Spine)

XTREME FACT – The earliest ichthyosaurs were shaped more like lizards with fins. Over time, they evolved into their fish-like shape.

On average, ichthyosaurs grew to lengths of 49 feet (15 m) and weighed about 2,000 pounds (907 kg). Their barrel-like bodies were equipped with stiff, paddle-like fins that gave them great speed and diving ability. Scientists guess that ichthyosaurs could reach speeds of 25 miles per hour (40 kph).

Ichthyosaurs died out 93 million years ago, long before other sea reptiles. This may have been caused by changes in ocean temperatures that resulted in a lack of oxygen. They also faced harsh competition for food. It's likely that sharks, who did not have to surface to breathe, took over their feeding areas.

PLESIOSAURS

Plesiosaurs had long necks and small heads. They lived 200 million to 65 million years ago. The name plesiosaur means "near lizard." When first discovered, it was thought that the bones were from an ancient lizard.

XTREME FACT – Scotland's Loch Ness monster was once believed to be a surviving plesiosaur. Unfortunately, the famous 1934 photo was discovered to be a hoax. It was a clay dinosaur head on a toy sub. No proof has been found that "Nessie" is alive.

Elasmosaurus
(Ribbon Lizard)

Muraenosaurus
(Moray Eel Lizard)

Muraenosaurus had a neck that was as long as its body and tail. It grew to a length of 20 feet (6 m). Its flipper-like limbs helped propel it through the water much like today's penguins. The powerful front limbs stroked, while its rear limbs steered and kept the long-necked sea reptile balanced.

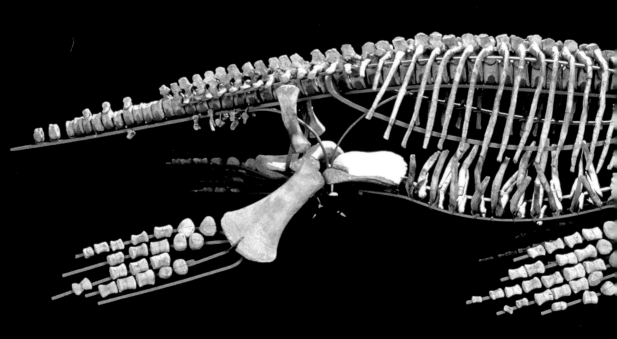

Cryptoclidus was a plesiosaur with unique teeth-filled jaws that closed together like a trap. It grew to a length of 13 feet (4 m). Some scientists believe this plesiosaur may have lived on the land and fed in the water. It would have moved much more easily in the sea.

Cryptoclidus
(Hidden Collarbone)

PLIOSAURS

Pliosaurs had short necks
and big heads. They lived
200 million to 80 million
years ago. These fierce
predators had huge jaws
and teeth. They fed on fish,
squid, sharks, and even
their smaller cousins, the
long-necked plesiosaurs.

**Liopleurodon
(Smooth-Sided Teeth)**

XTREME FACT – Liopleurodon reached a length of 39 feet (12 m). The huge pliosaur looked something like today's whales, except with long, sharp teeth.

Rhomaleosaurus was one of the largest pliosaurs living during the Jurassic period. Several nearly complete fossils of the 23-foot (7-m) -long pliosaur have been discovered in Europe. By studying the nasal cavities, it's believed these pliosaurs could smell blood in the water from a great distance. Much like today's sharks, they could find prey using their excellent sense of smell.

Mary Anning —
the fossil woman

Some of the finest fossils in this gallery were found by Mary Anning (1799–1847) of Lyme Regis, Dorset. At the age of 11, she discovered a complete ichthyosaur skeleton in the Blue Lias rocks of Charmouth beach. Fossil-hunting became a life-long passion, and Mary Anning earned respect from collectors and scientists alike. Sadly, the 'fossil woman' of Lyme Regis died of cancer at the age of 47.

Fossilized ichthyosaurs and plesiosaurs, preserved in Lower or Middle Jurassic rocks, have been found in many sites in southern England. Mary Anning is thought to be the first person to discover complete ichthyosaur and plesiosaur skeletons, and her remarkable fossils are still studied by scientists today.

Reproduction portrait of Mary Anning by an unknown artist.
Original presented by Miss Annette Anning in 1935.

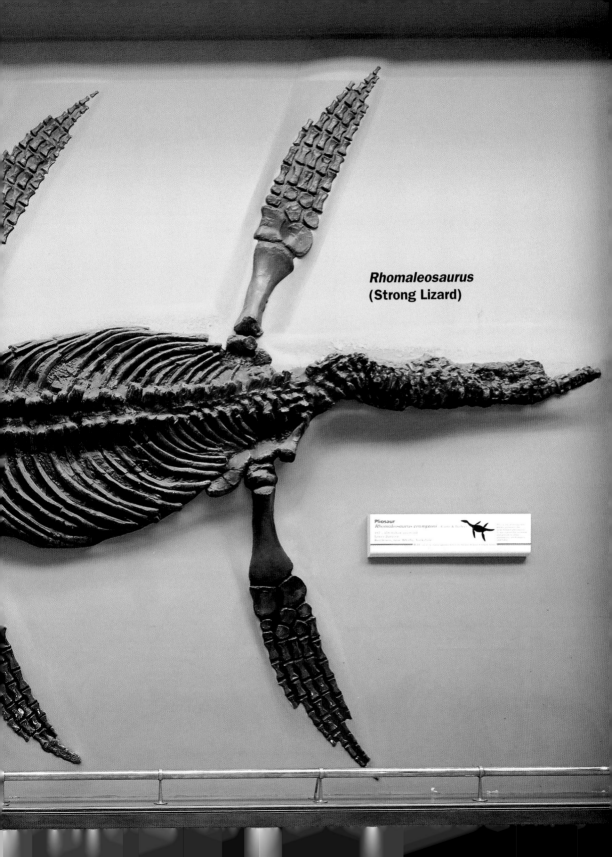

Rhomaleosaurus
(Strong Lizard)

Pliosaur
Rhomaleosaurus crompeoni

MOSASAURS

Mosasaurs had sleek bodies and long tails. They lived 90 to 65 million years ago. These sea reptiles are distant relatives of today's monitor lizards.

The name "mosasaur" comes from the Netherlands' Meuse River. It was in a limestone quarry near the river that the first fossils were found in 1764.

Tylosaurus grew up to 50 feet (15 m) in length. It was the largest of the mosasaurs. The smallest, *Dallasaurus*, was only 3 feet (.9 m) in length. Mosasaur fossils have been found all over the world.

Tylosaurus
(Knob Lizard)

Mosasaurs were powerful swimmers. They moved through the water by shifting their tails from side-to-side. They were not picky eaters, and feasted on everything from fish and turtles to sea birds.

XTREME FACT – *A mosasaur was one of the heroes of the 2015* Jurassic World *movie. However, the mosasaur was about twice as big in the movie as in real life.*

SEA REPTILE BIRTH

Sea reptiles did not lay eggs. Mothers gave live birth in water. We know this because fossil remains were found showing a baby emerging tail first from the mother's body. This is much like today's whales. Since sea reptiles were air breathers, the baby's head came out last in order to give the mother time to push the baby to the surface and keep it from drowning.

XTREME FACT– Sea reptile mothers usually gave birth to two or three babies. One fossilized female ichthyosaur, *Stenopterygius*, had seven babies inside her body.

A mosasaur mother gives birth.

EXTINCTION

About 66 million years ago, a world-changing event occurred. It may have been an asteroid or volcanic eruptions. It may have been climate change or diseases. Prehistoric animals began dying.

Ichthyosaurs had already died out about 90 million years ago. Pliosaurs died out 80 million years ago. After the extinction event, plesiosaurs and mosasaurs survived until 65 million years ago. They went extinct at the same time as the dinosaurs. Scientists continue to search for answers as to what killed the great masters of the ancient oceans, and all the prehistoric creatures of Earth's past.

GLOSSARY

EVOLVE
To change over time. Living things may change in shape, size, or other ways to make life better for future generations.

EXTINCT
When every member of a specific living thing has died. Sea reptiles are extinct.

FOSSILS
The preserved remains or imprints of prehistoric animals or plants in stone.

JURASSIC PERIOD
A time in Earth's history from 201 million to 145 million years ago. It's commonly referred to as the "age of the dinosaurs," as this is when large reptiles, sea life, and flowering plants all thrived.

MESOZOIC ERA
A time in Earth's history from about 245 million to 65 million years ago. Dinosaurs roamed the Earth at this time. This overall era includes the Triassic, Jurassic, and Cretaceous periods.

Nasal Cavity

The air-filled spaces behind the nose or nostril openings. This is the area where a creature's sense of smell is housed.

Quarry

A place where different types of stone are mined for use as building materials. Limestone, a whitish rock, is made up of the deposited remains of ancient marine animals and other minerals. Many excellent fossil finds have been discovered in limestone quarries.

Sclerotic Ring

A doughnut-shaped ring of bone that surrounds the eyes of many vertebrates (animals with backbones), except mammals (such as humans) and crocodilians. Ancient sea reptiles had well-developed sclerotic rings, which helped keep their eyes' shape even when diving into deep water or swimming at a fast speed. Without the sclerotic ring, both of these activities would have misshapen the eye and caused poor vision.

Online Resources

Booklinks
NONFICTION NETWORK
FREE! ONLINE NONFICTION RESOURCES

To learn more about Xtreme Dinosaurs, visit abdobooklinks.com. These links are routinely monitored and updated to provide the most current information available.

INDEX